Reading/Writing Companion

D1365137

Mc
Graw
Hill

mheducation.com/prek-12

Send all inquiries to:
McGraw Hill
1325 Avenue of the Americas
New York, NY 10019

ISBN: 978-1-26-572403-0
MHID: 1-26-572403-2

Printed in the United States of America.

3 4 5 6 7 8 9 LMN 26 25 24 23 22

A

Welcome to WONDERS!

We are so excited about how much you will learn and grow this year! We're here to help you set goals for your learning.

You will build on what you already know and learn new things every day.

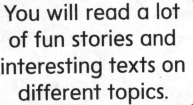

You will read a lot of fun stories and interesting texts on different topics.

You will write about the texts you read. You will also write texts of your own. You will do research as well.

You will explore new ideas by reading different texts.

Each week, we will set goals on the My Goals page. Here is an example:

I can read and understand realistic fiction.

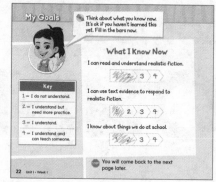

As you read and write, you will learn skills and strategies to help you reach your goals.

You will think about your learning and sometimes fill in a bar to show your progress.

Here are some questions you can ask yourself.

- Did I understand the task?

- Was it easy?

- Was it hard?

- What made it hard?

It is okay if I need more practice. The most important thing is to do my best and keep learning!

If you need more support, you can choose what to do.

- Talk to a friend or teacher.
- Use an Anchor Chart.
- Choose a center activity.

At the end of each week, you will complete a fun task to show what you have learned.

Then you will return to your My Goals page and think about your learning.

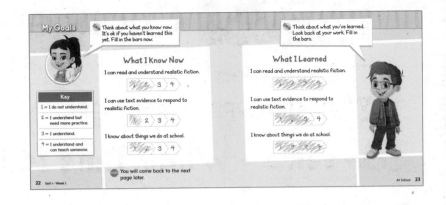

Unit 3 Changes Over Time

The Big Idea

Week 1 • What Time Is It?

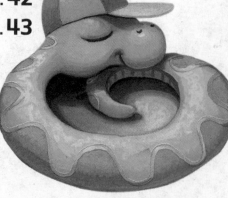

 Digital Tools *Find this eBook and other resources at:* **my.mheducation.com**

Week 2 • Watch It Grow!

Week 3 • Tales Over Time

Week 4 • Now and Then

andipantz/iStock/Getty Images

Week 5 • From Farm to Table

Extended Writing

Nonfiction

Connect and Reflect

Changes Over Time

 Listen to and think about the poem "Changes, Changes."

 Talk about the girl in the picture. What can she do that she could not do when she was younger?

The Big Idea

What can happen over time?

Build Knowledge

Build Vocabulary

 Talk with your partner about ways we can measure time.

 Write words about time.

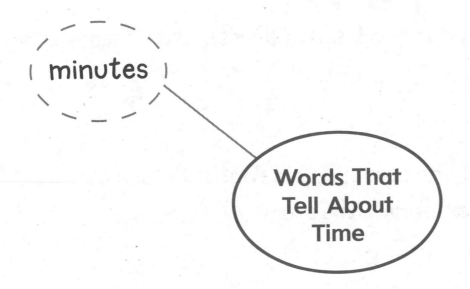

minutes

Words That
Tell About
Time

Ariel Skelley/Blend Images/Corbis

My Goals

 Think about what you know now. It will be fun to learn more. Fill in the bars.

Key

1 = I do not understand.
2 = I understand but need more practice.
3 = I understand.
4 = I understand and can teach someone.

What I Know Now

I can read and understand a fantasy story.

1 > 2 > 3 > 4 >

I can respond to a fantasy story by extending the story.

1 > 2 > 3 > 4 >

I know about ways we can measure time.

1 > 2 > 3 > 4 >

 You will come back to the next page later.

Think about what you've learned.
Keep trying. Fill in the bars.

What I Learned

I can read and understand a fantasy story.

1 2 3 4

I can respond to a fantasy story by extending the story.

1 2 3 4

I know about ways we can measure time.

1 2 3 4

Shared Read

How do we measure time?

My Goal

I can read and understand a fantasy story.

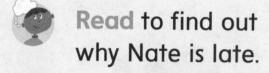 **Find Text Evidence**

Read to find out why Nate is late.

Circle the words with the same middle sound as *cake*.

Nate the Snake Is Late

Shared Read

 Find Text Evidence

 **Talk** about why Nate does not want to be late. What does this tell you about him?

 Talk about why Nate is not worried about the time on page 17.

It is 8 o'clock, and I can not be late.

I do not wish to make my pals wait.

I must be there at half past ten.

But I have lots of time until then.

Shared Read

 Find Text Evidence

 Underline and read aloud the words *way, some,* and *away*.

Talk about what Nate is doing. Predict what will happen because of his actions.

At last I am set and on my way there.

But I think I still have some time to spare.

I wade in this lake as frogs hop away.

I do not think they wish to play!

Find Text Evidence

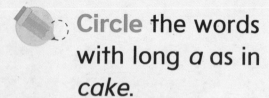

Circle the words with long *a* as in *cake*.

Talk about your prediction. Was it correct? Do you need to change it?

The sun is hot, and I nap on a rock.

Then I wake up and gaze at the clock.

Drats! It is 10 o'clock. Can it be?

Will my pals still be there for me?

Shared Read

 Underline and read aloud the words *why, now,* and *today*.

Retell the story using the pictures and words to help you.

I dash up a lane and past the gate.

I am on my way, but am I late?

My six best pals sit with Miss Tate.

I tell them all why I am late.

They grin at me and then they say,
"Now we can hear the story today!"

Writing Practice

Write Sentences

Nate the Snake Is Late

Talk about why Nate is late.

Listen to these sentences about running late.

> My dog gobbled up my homework. Then I was late for school!

Circle a strong verb.

Draw an arrow below the second sentence from the first word to the last word.

Writing Trait
Strong verbs help us know *how* something or someone moves.

24   Unit 3 · Week 1

Talk about a time you were late.

Write sentences about a time you were late. Use strong verbs.

_____

- -

_____

- -

_____

- -

_____

 Circle the strong verbs you used.

 Draw an arrow below one sentence from the first word to the last word.

Check In | 1 | 2 | 3 | 4

A **fantasy** story has made-up characters.
Fantasy stories can be told in first-person
using the words *I, me, my,* and *we.*

Nate the Snake Is Late

 Reread to find out who is telling this
fantasy story.

 Talk about who is telling the story and
how you know.

 Write the words that tell you who is
telling the story. Draw the character.

Check In 1 2 3 4

Words That Tell	Character

Events are things that happen in a story. Events take place in the beginning, middle, and end of a story.

 Reread "Nate the Snake Is Late."

 Talk about what happens in the beginning of the story.

 Write about the events of the story.

Check In 1 > 2 > 3 > 4 >

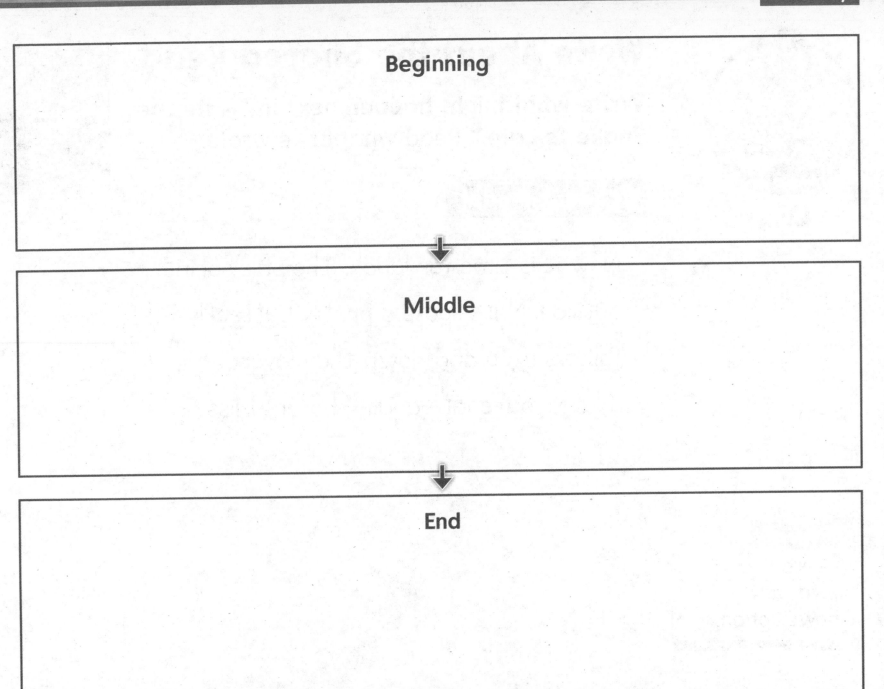

Beginning

Middle

End

Writing and Grammar

Luke

Write About the Shared Read

Write what might happen next in "Nate the Snake Is Late." Read what Luke wrote.

Student Model

Now it is time for lunch. The pals sprint outside. Nate spots a pretty butterfly. He follows it up and down the playground. "Nate, you're late again!" hollers Miss Tate.

Polka Dot/Getty Images Plus/Getty Images

Grammar

A **verb** is a word that shows action.

Talk about details Luke used from the story. Underline any strong verbs.

Circle the verb in the fourth sentence.

Draw an arrow below the fourth sentence from the first word to the last word.

Write what you notice about Luke's writing.

Quick Tip

You can talk about Luke's writing using these sentence starters:

I noticed . . .
Luke used . . .

Respond to the **Anchor Text**

 Retell the story in your own words.

 Write about the story.

Why does the bus stop for the apes
and the duck?

_____

- -

_____

_____

- -

_____

Text Evidence

Page

Why does the bus make one last stop
before school?

_____

- -

_____

_____

- -

_____

Text Evidence

Page

Check In   1 2 3 4

Talk about what is happening on page 10.

 Write two clues that help you know who tells the story.

Clue from Text	Clue from Pictures

How does the author let you know who is telling the story?

_____

- -

_____

- -

_____

 Talk about the sentences with rhyming words on pages 12–13.

Write pairs of rhyming words from the story.

Page 12	Page 13

What feeling does the story have because of the rhyming words?

_____

- -

_____

- -

_____

Talk about the things that happen in the story on page 18.

 Write about two of the things that happen.

1.
2.

Why did the boy say these things happened?

_____

- -

_____

_____

- - - - - - - - - - - - - - - - - -

Writing and Grammar

My Goal I can respond to a fantasy story by extending the story.

Write About the Anchor Text

Write four more pages of the story. Tell the excuses the boy might give his mom for getting home late.

 Talk about the question.

 Write your answer below.

On My Way to School
by Wong Herbert Yee

Remember:

☐ Use strong verbs to help readers.

☐ Turn the line in your writing.

☐ Use verbs correctly.

Check In 1 > 2 > 3 > 4 >

It's About Time!

Some clocks have faces with hands. The hands point to the numbers. Some clocks have just numbers.

All clocks tell the hour and minute. There are 60 minutes in an hour. There are 60 seconds in a minute.

 Read to find out about telling time.

 Underline the sentence that explains how all clocks are the same.

Talk about why the author included two different photos on this page.

(t)McGraw-Hill Education; (b)Stockbyte/Getty Images

What Time Is It? **37**

Long ago, people didn't have clocks. They used the Sun to tell time instead. Tools like sundials helped them. The Sun's shadow showed the hour. But people had to guess the minutes. What time is this sundial showing?

Underline the word that tells what people used before clocks.

Circle what is needed for a sundial to work.

Talk about why the author included information about sundials. How is this different from the information on page 37?

Quick Tip

Look at the Sun's shadow in the photo. What will happen when the Sun moves?

David J. Green/Alamy Stock Photo

Talk about the information in the text.

 Write what the facts are mostly about on pages 37 and 38.

Page 37	Page 38

Why is "It's About Time!" a good title for this text?

_____

- -

_____

- -

_____

Talk About It

What does the author want you to know after reading this text?

Check In 1 2 3 4

Interview About Your Day

Step 1 **Pick** a classmate to ask about his or her usual day.

_____

- -

_____

Step 2 **Decide** what you want to know about your classmate's day. Write your questions.

_____

- -

_____

_____

- -

_____

_____

- -

_____

Step 3 **Ask** your questions.

Step 4 Write what you learned about each part of your classmate's day.

Parts of My Classmate's Day	What Usually Happens

Step 5 Choose how to present your work.

Check In 1 > 2 > 3 > 4 >

Talk about why the bird in this poem says what he says.

Compare this poem to the beginning of *On My Way to School.*

> **Quick Tip**
>
> Compare the story and poem using these sentence starters:
>
> *The boy in the story . . .*
>
> *The person telling the poem is also . . .*

Time to Rise

A birdie with a yellow bill
Hopped upon my window sill,
Cocked his shining eye and said:
"Ain't you 'shamed, you
sleepy-head!"

— Robert Louis Stevenson

Check In | 1 | 2 | 3 | 4

Write Tips for Being on Time

1 **Look** at your Build Knowledge pages in your reader's notebook. What did you learn about ways we measure time?

2 **Think** about two of the characters you read about. Why were they late? Write a list of tips to help them be on time in the future. Use text evidence. Use two vocabulary words from the Word Bank.

3 **Draw** a picture to go with your tips.

Think about what you learned this week. Fill in the bars on page 13.

Build Knowledge

? Essential Question **How do plants change as they grow?**

44 Unit 3 · Week 2

Build Vocabulary

 Talk with your partner about plants that you know.

 Write words about plants.

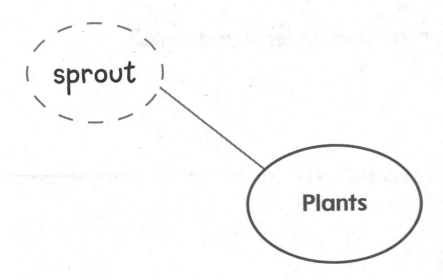

sprout

Plants

Masterfile

My Goals

 Think about what you know now. It's important to keep learning. Fill in the bars.

Key

1 =	I do not understand.
2 =	I understand but need more practice.
3 =	I understand.
4 =	I understand and can teach someone.

What I Know Now

I can read and understand a play.

1 > 2 > 3 > 4

I can respond to a play by extending the play.

1 > 2 > 3 > 4

I know about how plants change as they grow.

1 > 2 > 3 > 4

 You will come back to the next page later.

What I Learned

I can read and understand a play.

1 > 2 > 3 > 4 >

I can respond to a play by extending the play.

1 > 2 > 3 > 4 >

I know about how plants change as they grow.

1 > 2 > 3 > 4 >

My Goal

I can read and understand a play.

Find Text Evidence

Read to find out what happens when it is time to plant.

Find the title. Point to each word as you read it. What do you think this play is about?

Essential Question

? How do plants change as they grow?

Time to Plant!

Watch It Grow! **49**

🔍 **Find Text Evidence**

 Talk about what the characters say. Make a prediction about what will happen next.

 Underline and read aloud the word *together*.

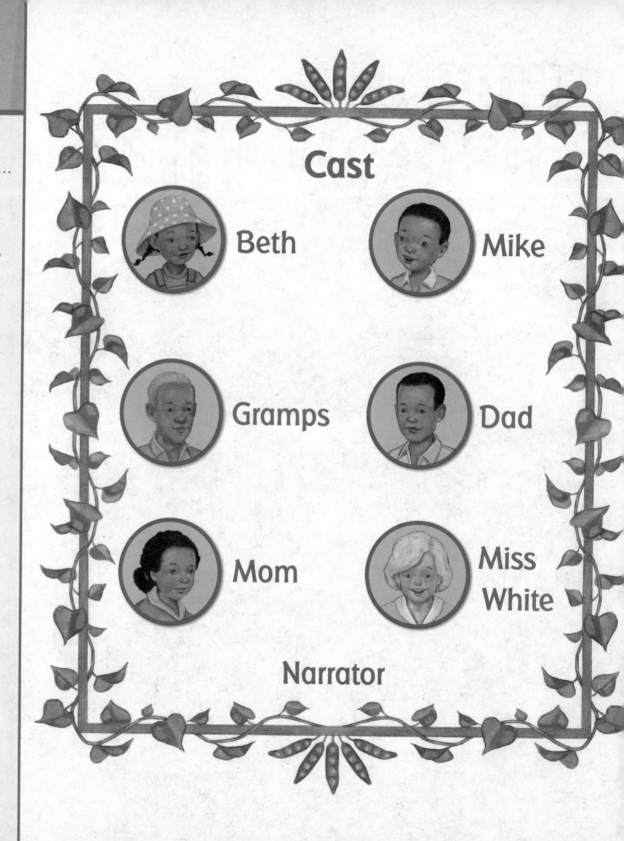

Cast

Beth

Mike

Gramps

Dad

Mom

Miss White

Narrator

Beth: Dad, can we plant a garden?

Dad: Yes! That will be fine!

Gramps: We can plant vegetables.

Mike: Yum! Let's do it together.

Play

Shared Read

Find Text Evidence

🖊 Underline and read aloud the words *green, water,* and *grow.*

👥 Think about what the characters say. Talk about your prediction. Correct it if you need to.

Mom:	Dad and I will dig.
Mike:	I will drop in five seeds.
Gramps:	I will set in green plants.
Beth:	And I will get water!

Narrator: Days pass. The Sun shines.
Rain plinks and plunks.

Beth: I can spot buds on the vines!

Dad: Sun and water made
them grow.

Shared Read

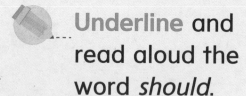
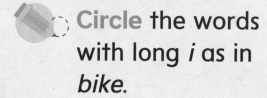

Narrator: Days pass. The Sun shines. Rain drips and drops.

Beth: The vegetables got big!

Dad: We should pick them.

Mom: Yes, it's time!

Play

Mike: I like to munch while I pick. I will take a bite. Yum!

Gramps: Sun and water made them ripe.

Shared Read

 Talk about Beth and Mike. Did they get what they expected?

 Retell the story using the pictures and words to help you.

Narrator: They pick piles and piles.

Beth: Yikes! That's a lot!

Mike: We can't eat them all.

Gramps: I think I have a plan.

Play

Mike: This bag is for you.

Miss White: They are such pretty vegetables! Thank you!

Beth: Sun and water made them grow.

Writing Practice

Write Sentences

Talk about the foods that Beth and Mike grow.

Listen to these sentences about growing.

If I had a garden, I would grow spinach. Spinach is green and tastes yummy.

Underline the sensory details.

Circle the word "I."

Talk about what you would grow.

Write sentences about what you would grow. Use sensory details.

_____

- -

_____

- -

_____

Underline sensory details you used.

Circle the word "I."

Writing Skill

Remember, the word **I** is always capitalized.

| Check In | 1 | 2 | 3 | 4 |

A **play** is a genre. A play is a story that is meant to be performed. It has dialogue, or words that characters speak, and a setting. It often has a narrator who tells the story.

 Reread to find out what makes this story a play.

 Talk about how you know it is a play. Then describe the setting.

 Write something you learn about Beth and Mike from the dialogue.

Check In 1 2 3 4

Character	What I Learned From the Dialogue

Events in a story or play happen in a certain order, or sequence. The sequence of events is what happens first, next, then, and last in a story.

 Reread "Time to Plant!"

 Talk about what happens first, next, then, and last in the play.

 Write what happens in the correct sequence.

Check In 1 2 3 4

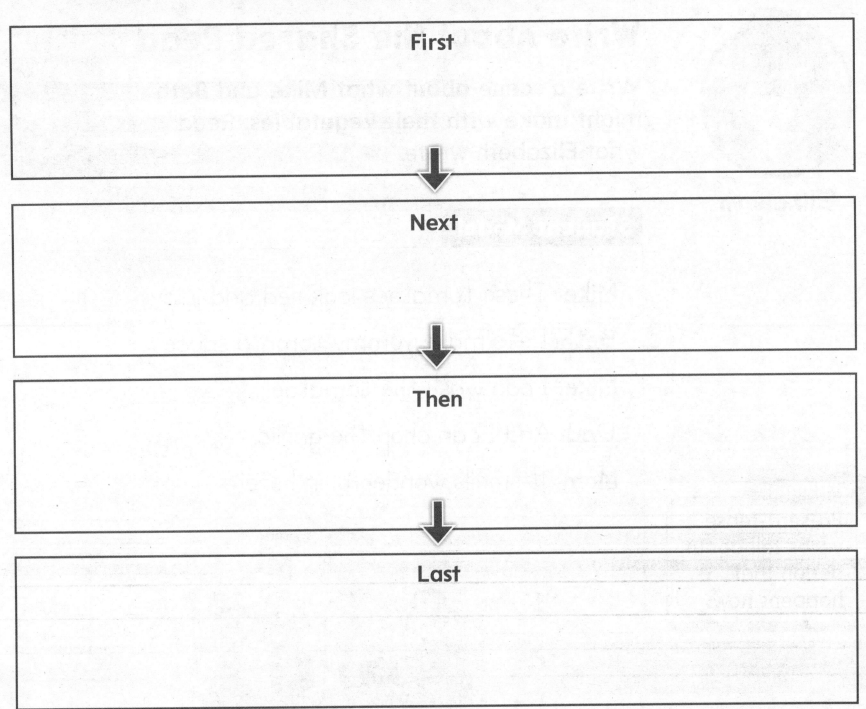

First

Next

Then

Last

Writing and Grammar

Elizabeth

Write About the Shared Read

Write a scene about what Mike and Beth might make with their vegetables. Read what Elizabeth wrote.

Time to Plant!

Student Model

<u>Mike</u>: These tomatoes look red and juicy.

<u>Beth</u>: Let's make yummy tomato sauce.

<u>Mike</u>: I can wash the tomatoes.

<u>Dad</u>: And I can chop the garlic.

<u>Mom</u>: It smells wonderful in here!

Grammar

Present-tense verbs tell about action that happens now.

Talk about details Elizabeth used from the story. Underline the sensory details.

Circle the present-tense verb in the fifth line.

Draw a box around the word <u>I</u>.

Write what you notice about Elizabeth's writing.

Quick Tip

You can use these sentence starters:

I noticed . . .
Elizabeth used . . .

_____

- -

_____

_____

- -

_____

_____

- -

_____

 Retell the play in the right sequence.

 Write about the play.

Why does Lola's family help tug the
yuca plant?

_____

- -

_____

_____

- -

_____

Text Evidence

Page

How do you think Paco feels when Rat's
plan works?

_____

- -

_____

_____

- -

_____

Text Evidence

Page

Check In 1 2 3 4

Talk about the characters' feelings on pages 32–33.

 Write about the characters' feelings.

Ana says . . .	→	She feels . . .
Mom says . . .	→	She feels . . .

How does the author help you know the characters' feelings?

_____

_____

_____

 Talk about what Lola says and does on pages 32 and 36.

✏️ **Write** clues from the play that show what Lola likes.

On page 32, Lola . . .	On page 36, Lola . . .

What does Lola like to do?

_____

_____

_____

_____

Talk about what Rat says on page 41.

 Write what you know about Rat.

When . . .	it helps me know . . .
Rat says:	

How does the dialogue help you learn about the characters?

_____

- - - - - - - - - - - - - - - - - - - -

_____

_____

- - - - - - - - - - - - - - - - - - - -

_____

Writing and Grammar

Write About the Anchor Text

Think of a different animal that might have been able to help get the yuca plant out. Write a scene where he/she helps out.

 Talk about the question.

 Write your answer below.

Remember:

☐ Use sensory details.

☐ Capitalize the word **I**.

☐ Use present-tense verbs correctly.

Check In 1 2 3 4

How Plants Grow

When a seed is planted, a root grows down in the soil. The root holds the seed in the soil. It takes in water, too.

The stem grows up from the seed. When it pops out of the soil, it is called a sprout. Green leaves grow on the stem.

 Read to find out how plants grow.

 Underline two ways that the root helps a plant.

 Talk about how the photo helps you understand the meaning of the word *sprout*.

Nic Miller/Alamy Stock Photo

Over time, blossoms pop up on the plant. These blossoms are the plant's flowers. They can grow into a fruit such as this pumpkin. Many fruits can grow on one plant vine.

Inside the fruit are seeds. These seeds can be used to grow new plants.

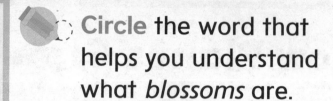 **Circle** the word that helps you understand what *blossoms* are.

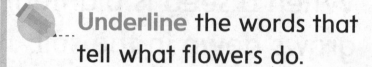 **Underline** the words that tell what flowers do.

Talk about why the author included the photo and labels on this page.

blossom

fruit

msgrafixx/Shutterstock.com

Quick Tip

Think about how the labels help you understand the photo.

Talk about the sequence of the text.

 Write the sequence.

First, a seed . . .

Next, the seed . . .

Then, the plant . . .

Last, these can . . .

How is the information in this text organized?

_____

- -

_____

- -

_____

Talk About It

What would be
another good title
for this text?

Check In 1 ⟩ 2 ⟩ 3 ⟩ 4 ⟩

From Seed to Plant

Step 1 **Pick** a plant to research.

_____

- -

_____

Step 2 **Write** questions about your plant and what
it needs to grow.

_____

- -

_____

_____

- -

_____

_____

- -

_____

Step 3 **Find** books or websites with the information
you need. Read for answers to your questions.

Step 4 **List** what you learned about your plant's needs.

_____

- - - - - - - - - - - - - - - - - - -

_____

- - - - - - - - - - - - - - - - - - -

_____

- - - - - - - - - - - - - - - - - - -

_____

- - - - - - - - - - - - - - - - - - -

_____

- - - - - - - - - - - - - - - - - - -

_____

- - - - - - - - - - - - - - - - - - -

_____

Step 5 **Draw** your plant and label the parts.

Step 6 **Choose** how to present your work.

| Check In | 1 | 2 | 3 | 4 |

Make Connections

 Talk about why *The Life of a Pomegranate* would be a good title for this painting.

 Compare a pomegranate to the other plants you read about in "Time to Plant!"

Quick Tip

Compare using these sentence starters:

A pomegranate has . . .

Other plants also have . . .

This painting shows pomegranate seeds, tree, blossoms, and fruit.

Check In 1 > 2 > 3 > 4 >

Show Your Knowledge

Draw Growing Plants

1 **Look** at your Build Knowledge pages in your reader's notebook. What types of plants did you learn about?

2 **Choose** three of the plants you read about. Draw each of them when they are little. Then, draw the plants when they are big.

3 **Write** about how the plants changed. Use text evidence. Use two of your vocabulary words from the Word Bank.

Think about what you learned this week. Fill in the bars on page 47.

Essential Question What is a folktale?

Build Vocabulary

 Talk with your partner about folktales you know.

 Write words about folktales.

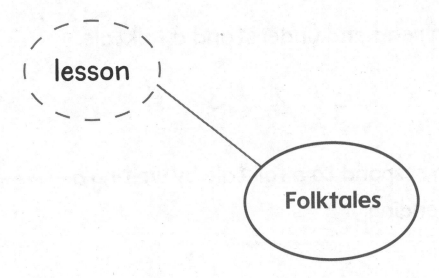

lesson

Folktales

Adam Taylor/Digital Vision/Getty Images

My Goals

 Think about what you know now. It's important to do your best. Fill in the bars.

What I Know Now

I can read and understand a folktale.

| 1 | 2 | 3 | 4 |

I can respond to a folktale by writing a new ending.

| 1 | 2 | 3 | 4 |

I know about different folktales.

| 1 | 2 | 3 | 4 |

Key

1 = I do not understand.

2 = I understand but need more practice.

3 = I understand.

4 = I understand and can teach someone.

 You will come back to the next page later.

Think about what you've learned. What helped you the most? Fill in the bars.

What I Learned

I can read and understand a folktale.

| 1 | 2 | 3 | 4 |

I can respond to a folktale by writing a new ending.

| 1 | 2 | 3 | 4 |

I know about different folktales.

| 1 | 2 | 3 | 4 |

Shared Read

My Goal

I can read and understand a folktale.

Find Text Evidence

 Read to find out what makes the mitten nice.

Find the title. Point to and read aloud each word in the title.

Essential Question

? **What is a folktale?**

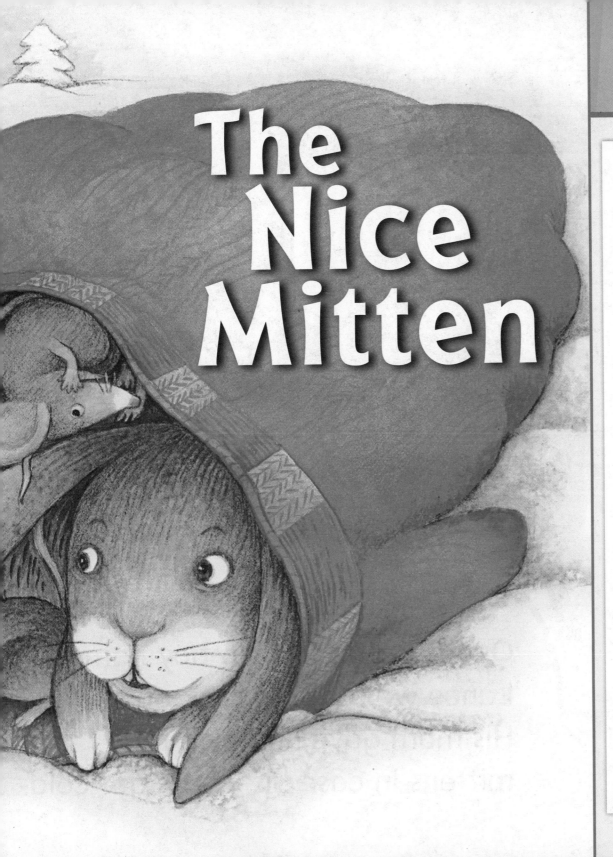

The Nice Mitten

🔍 Find Text Evidence

⭕ Circle the words with the soft *c* sound as in *race*.

___ Underline and read aloud the word *upon*.

Once upon a time, a boy named Lance went out to pick up sticks. His mom gave him nice red mittens in case his hands got cold.

"Take the mittens and keep them safe," his mom said. But as Lance left, he ran fast and lost a mitten at the edge of the wide forest.

Shared Read

🔍 **Find Text Evidence**

✏️ **Underline** and read aloud the words *so* and *happy*.

👫 **Talk** about why the mitten puffed up a bit.

Five mice saw the mitten. "This is a nice place to rest," they said. So the happy mice went in and rested.

Then, a rabbit raced by. "This is
a nice place for hiding," she said.
So the rabbit went in and hid.
The mitten puffed up a bit.

Shared Read

🔍 **Find Text Evidence**

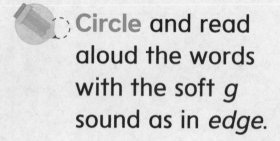

✏️ **Circle** and read aloud the words with the soft *g* sound as in *edge*.

👧👦 **Talk** about what has happened to the mitten so far. Make a prediction about what will happen to it next.

Next, a hedgehog came sniffing by. "This is a nice place for taking a nap," he said. So the hedgehog went in and slept. The mitten puffed up a bit more.

Just then, a big bear came by. "This is a nice place to get warm," he said. So the big bear went in. The mitten puffed up from all the animals in it. It puffed up as much as a mitten can.

Find Text Evidence

Talk about what happened to the mitten. Did you predict this?

Retell the story using the pictures and words to help you.

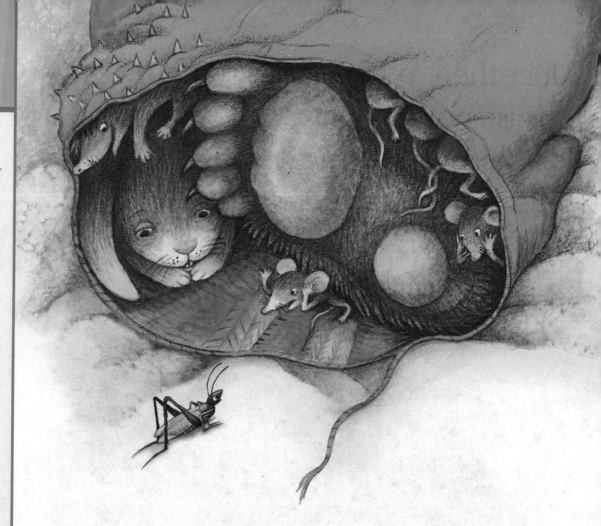

At last, a black cricket came by. "This is a nice place," he said.

"We do not have any space," said the animals in the mitten.

But the black cricket went in. And just as he did . . .

Rip! Snap! POP!

When Lance came back, there was not a trace of red mitten left. So sad!

Writing Practice

Write Sentences

 Talk about what happens to Lance's mitten.

 Listen to these sentences about a lost pet.

> I looked for my lost hamster everywhere. He was under my desk the whole time!

Underline a specific word that tells what was lost.

Circle a word that ends with **-ed** or **-ing**.

Writing Trait

Specific words are words that tell exactly what you mean.

Talk about something you lost.

Write sentences about what happened to something you lost. Use specific words.

_____

- -

_____

- -

_____

- -

_____

Underline the specific words you used.

Circle any words that end in **-ed** or **-ing**.

Writing Skill

The ending **-ed** tells about the past.

The ending **-ing** tells about the present.

Check In 1 ⟩ 2 ⟩ 3 ⟩ 4 ⟩

Shared Read

A **folktale** is a story that has been told for many years. Folktales may have animal characters that act like people. It can have a moral, or lesson.

 Reread to find out what makes this story a folktale.

 Talk about the words "Once upon a time." What do they mean?

 Write two clues from the story that show it is a folktale.

Check In 1 2 3 4

Folktale Clues

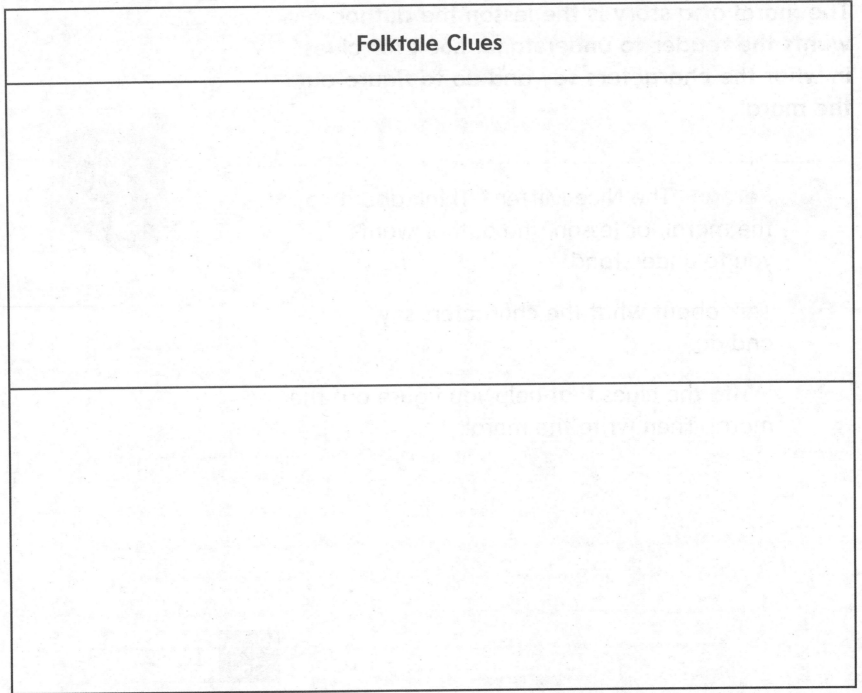

The **moral** of a story is the lesson the author wants the reader to understand. Look for clues in what the characters say and do to figure out the moral.

 Reread "The Nice Mitten." Think about the moral, or lesson, the author wants you to understand.

 Talk about what the characters say and do.

 Write the clues that help you figure out the moral. Then write the moral.

Check In 1 2 3 4

Clue

Clue

Moral

Writing and Grammar

Anna

Write About the Shared Read

Write a new story about a boy who loses his boot. Read what Anna wrote.

The Nice Mitten

Grammar

Past-tense verbs tell about actions in the past. **Future-tense verbs** tell about actions that will happen in the future.

Student Model

Once upon a time, a boy lost his boot in sticky mud.

A little chipmunk walked by the boot.

"How nice and warm," she said.

And she hopped into her new home!

Talk about details Anna used. Underline the specific word that tells who lost a boot.

Circle the past-tense verbs in the second and fourth sentences.

Write what you notice about Anna's writing.

 Retell the folktale in your own words.

 Write about the folktale.

Why do Gram and Gramps chase after the
Gingerbread Man?

_____

- -

_____

_____

- -

Text Evidence

Page

Why does the Gingerbread Man stop for the fox?

_____

- -

_____

_____

- -

_____

Text Evidence

Page

Check In   1 2 3 4

Talk about which words repeat on pages 56 and 6I.

Write the sentences with repeating words. Then read them aloud with your partner.

How do the repeating words affect the story? Share your answer.

_____

- -

_____

- -

_____

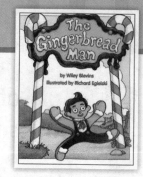

 Talk about what happens when the Gingerbread Man meets the cow and the duck on pages 57–60.

Write about each event.

Gingerbread Man Meets the Cow	Gingerbread Man Meets the Duck

What do you notice about the pattern in the story?

_____

- -

_____

_____

- -

_____

Talk about what happens when the Gingerbread Man meets the fox on page 61.

 Write about the event.

Gingerbread Man Meets the Fox

How does the pattern in the story change?

_____

- -

_____

_____

- -

_____

Check In 1 2 3 4

Writing and Grammar

Write About the Anchor Text

Imagine the Gingerbread Man had chosen to go around the lake. Then write a new ending to the story.

 Talk about the question.

 Write your answer below.

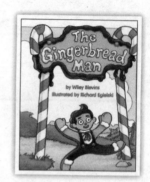

Remember:

☐ Use specific words.

☐ Use -ed and -ing correctly.

☐ Use past-tense verbs correctly.

Check In 1 〉 2 〉 3 〉 4

Drakestail

There once was a duck named Drakestail. He was a kind and patient duck. One day, the king asked Drakestail if he could borrow some money.

Drakestail waited for the king to pay him back. But the king did not. So, Drakestail set off to see the king.

Read to find out the moral of this folktale.

Talk about how the author shows that Drakestail is a kind and patient duck.

On his way, he saw Fox, Pond, and Hive. Drakestail's three friends hopped into his bag. They wanted to help Drakestail.

They finally got to the palace. Drakestail asked, "Can I have my money back?"

"I already spent your money," said the greedy king. "Guards, stick that duck in the hen pen!"

Underline why Fox, Pond, and Hive hopped into Drakestail's bag.

Talk about what the picture helps you understand about Drakestail's new friends.

Quick Tip

You can use this sentence starter:

The picture shows me …

"Fox! Come and help me!" yelled Drakestail. Fox chased the hens away.

"Guards, cook that duck for dinner!" the king yelled.

The guards lit a fire under a big pot. But, just in time, Pond burst out of the bag. She quickly put out the fire. Drakestail ran!

 Underline what Fox does to help Drakestail.

 Circle the words that tell you how the king spoke. What does this tell you about how the king was feeling?

"Get that duck!"
cried the king.

But Hive popped
out of the bag.
A swarm of bees chased the
king out of the palace.

"Wow! Drakestail should be
our king!" said the townsfolk.

Drakestail sang,
"I will be the
king today,
if you say my
friends can stay!"

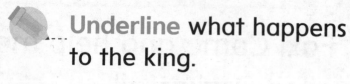

Underline what happens
to the king.

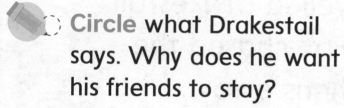

Circle what Drakestail
says. Why does he want
his friends to stay?

Talk about what you learned from "Drakestail."

Write what you learned about friends from this folktale.

Fox helped by ...	Pond helped by ...	Hive helped by ...

What is the moral of this folktale?

_____

_____

_____

Talk About It

Talk about how Fox, Pond, and Hive helped Drakestail. Talk about some ways Drakestail could be a good friend to them in return.

Check In 1 > 2 > 3 > 4 >

All About a Folktale

Step 1 Find a folktale you have never heard or read. Look online or in books.

Step 2 Read or listen to the folktale.

Step 3 Write the title of the folktale. Then write what it is about.

_____

- -

_____

_____

- -

_____

- -

_____

- -

_____

Step 4 Write why you think people have been telling the folktale for years and years.

_____

- -

_____

- -

_____

- -

_____

Step 5 Choose how to present your work.

_____

- -

_____

- -

_____

Check In 1 2 3 4

Talk about how the wolf might trick the girl in the picture.

Compare the characters in the picture to the characters from *The Gingerbread Man*.

In *Little Red Riding Hood*, the wolf tries to trick the girl.

Quick Tip

You can compare the characters using these sentence starters:

In The Gingerbread Man, *the characters* . . .

In Little Red Riding Hood, *a character* . . .

Check In 1 2 3 4

Write Your Opinion

1 **Look** at your Build Knowledge pages in your reader's notebook. What did you learn about folktales?

2 **Write** your opinion about why people should read folktales. Include reasons for your opinion. Include examples from the texts. Use two vocabulary words from the Word Bank.

3 **Draw** a picture of one of the folktales you wrote about. Include a caption.

Think about what you learned this week. Fill in the bars on page 81.

Build Knowledge

Essential Question How is life different than it was long ago?

Build Vocabulary

 Talk with your partner about how life was different long ago.

 Write words about long ago.

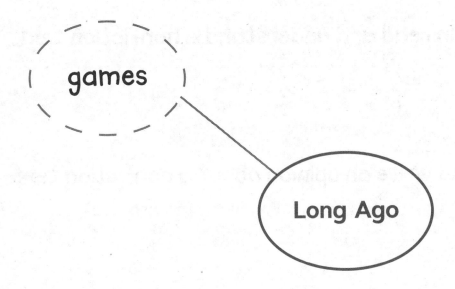

games

Long Ago

Fox Photos/Stringer/Hulton Archive/Getty Images

My Goals

 Think about what you know now. Everyone learns more with practice. Fill in the bars.

What I Know Now

I can read and understand a nonfiction text.

> 1 > 2 > 3 > 4 >

I can write an opinion about a nonfiction text.

> 1 > 2 > 3 > 4 >

I know about how life was different long ago.

> 1 > 2 > 3 > 4 >

Key	
1 =	I do not understand.
2 =	I understand but need more practice.
3 =	I understand.
4 =	I understand and can teach someone.

 You will come back to the next page later.

Think about what you've learned.
What helped you do your best?
Fill in the bars.

What I Learned

I can read and understand a nonfiction text.

1   2   3   4

I can write an opinion about a nonfiction text.

1   2   3   4

I know about how life was different long ago.

1   2   3   4

Shared Read

My Goal

I can read and understand a nonfiction text.

Find Text Evidence

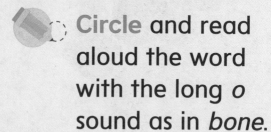

Read to find out how life at home is different than it was long ago.

Circle and read aloud the word with the long *o* sound as in *bone*.

Essential Question

How is life different than it was long ago?

Life at Home

Find Text Evidence

Underline and read aloud the word *people*.

Think about what you just read. Do you understand it? Reread to be sure.

Has home life changed a lot since long ago?

Yes, it has!

Long ago, many families cooked, worked, and slept in one room.

Today, families can live in large homes that have lots of space.

A long time ago, homes had just one room. People ate and slept in that same room.

Today, homes can have many rooms.

Shared Read

🔍 **Find Text Evidence**

Circle the words with long *u* as in *cute*.

Talk about how people used to cook. Reread and use the picture if you are not sure.

How did people cook and bake long ago?

A home had a brick fireplace with a pole. A huge pot hung on this pole. People cooked in this big pot.

Long ago, there was an oven at the side of the fireplace. Bread was baked there.

Today, stoves can use gas or electricity.

Now, we use a stove
to cook and bake things.
We still use pots.
But these pots are not
as big as that old pot!

🔍 **Find Text Evidence**

✏️ **Underline** and read aloud the words *boy* and *girl*.

👫 **Talk** about helping out at home long ago and today. Which was easier?

Back then, kids helped out a lot. A boy helped his dad plant crops. A girl helped her mom inside the home. She made socks and caps. It takes a long time to make those things.

A spinning wheel was used to spin wool into yarn.

Today, people buy most of the things they need and want.

Now, we shop for things such as socks and caps. We shop for things to eat, as well.

But kids still help out at home.

Shared Read

Talk about why washing dishes is easier today. Reread and use the pictures if you are not sure.

Retell the text using pictures, photos, and words to help you.

Back then, people got water from a well. Then they filled up a big tub and washed things.

In the past, people washed dishes in a tub made of wood.

Now, people can wash things in a sink. We can wash dishes in a dishwasher, too.

Life is not as hard today as it was long ago!

Today, it's easy to wash dishes in a sink or dishwasher.

Write Sentences

 Talk about how people lived long ago.

 Listen to these sentences about life at home today.

Today, we have things that help us. We have stoves, sinks, and dishwashers.

 Underline the idea the author wants the reader to know.

 Circle any words from your Word Bank.

Writing Trait

Focus on one idea to help readers understand what you are trying to say.

Talk about what life was like long ago.

Write your opinion about life long ago.
Make sure you focus on one idea.

_____

- -

_____

- -

_____

- -

_____

Underline the idea you focused on.

Circle any words from your Word Bank.

Writing Skill

Remember, you can use your Word Bank to help you spell words.

Check In 1 2 3 4

A **nonfiction** text gives information
and facts about real people and real things.

 Reread to find out about the real things
this nonfiction text tells about.

 Talk about what this text tells about.

Write about two real things in the text.
Then write what you learn about them.

Check In 1 > 2 > 3 > 4 >

Real Things	What I Learn

Authors often include details that show how things are the same or different to explain something in the text. When you compare, you think about how things are the same. When you contrast, you think about how things are different.

 Reread "Life at Home."

 Talk about how homes long ago and today are alike and different.

 Write about homes long ago and now.

Check In | 1 > 2 > 3 > 4 >

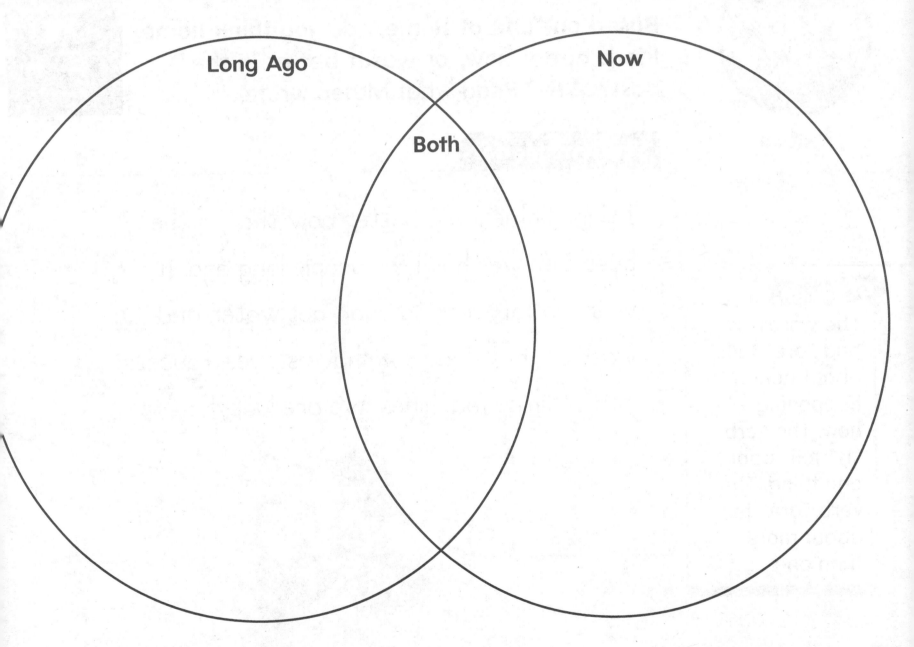

Long Ago

Now

Both

Writing and Grammar

Mateo

Grammar

The words "is" and "are" tell about action happening now. The verb "is" tells about one thing. The verb "are" tells about more than one.

Write About the Shared Read

Based on "Life at Home," do you think home life is better now, or was it better in the past? Why? Read what Mateo wrote.

Student Model

I think home life is better now than in the past. Life was hard for people long ago. It was a lot of work to cook, get water, and wash clothes. Today, we have stoves, faucets, and washing machines. We are lucky!

Talk about details Mateo used from the text. Underline the idea Mateo wants the reader to know.

Circle the words "is" and "are."

Draw a box around any words from your Word Bank in the second sentence.

Write what you notice about Mateo's writing.

Quick Tip

You can talk about Mateo's writing using these sentence starters:

I noticed . . .
Mateo used . . .

 Retell the text in your own words.

 Write about the text.

How did children long ago get water?

_____

- -

_____

- -

_____

Text Evidence

Page

Why are kids today more likely to want to
help clean clothes than they were long ago?

_____

- -

_____

- -

_____

Text Evidence

Page

Check In 1 2 3 4

Talk about what you learn from the text on pages 76–77.

Write about the photos on pages 76–77.

Page 76	Page 77

How does the author organize the information?

_____

- -

_____

- -

_____

 Talk about what you see in the photos on pages 78–79.

 Write what the photos show.

Page 78	Page 79

How do the photos help you understand the information in the text?

_____

- -

_____

- -

_____

Talk about the details on page 80.
Then talk about the details on page 81.

 Write details from the text and photos.

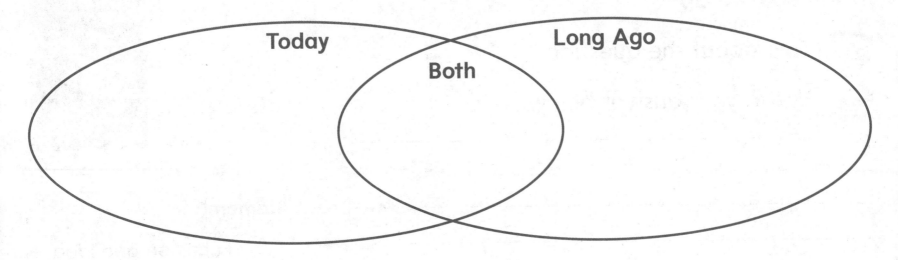

Today   Both   Long Ago

What do you understand because of the way the author organizes the information and details?

_____

- -

_____

- -

Check In   1   2   3   4

Writing and Grammar

Write About the Anchor Text

Based on *Long Ago and Now*, do you think being a kid is better now, or was it better in the past? Why?

 Talk about the question.

 Write your answer below.

_____

_____

_____

_____

_____

_____

_____

_____

_____

_____

Remember:

☐ Focus on one idea.

☐ Use words from your Word Bank.

☐ Use the words *is* and *are* correctly.

Check In 1 2 3 4

From Horse to Plane

People today can go places in cars, planes, and trains. Long ago there were not as many kinds of transportation. Before engines, people had to walk or use horses.

 Read to find out how transportation has changed.

 Circle the words that tell how we can go places today.

 Talk about why the author included the photo on this page. How does it help you understand the text?

Then the train was invented. Years later, cars were invented. Soon, the airplane was invented.

Airplanes can go over mountains and oceans. Today we can go across the world in a day. That could take years long ago!

 Circle the kinds of transportation that came after horses.

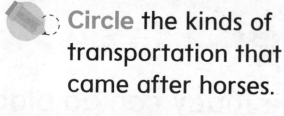 **Talk** about how the author feels about the invention of airplanes. How do you know?

Quick Tip

Use these sentence starters:

The author …
I know this because …

Bettmann/Getty Images

Talk about the information on each page.

 Compare how people went places long ago and now.

Long Ago	Now

Why is "From Horse to Plane" a good title for this text?

_____

- -

_____

- -

_____

Talk About It

What does the author want you to learn from reading this text?

Check In 1 ⟩ 2 ⟩ 3 ⟩ 4

Interview About Long Ago

Step 1 **Pick** a teacher or an older person at school to ask about his or her school life as a child.

_____

- -

_____

Step 2 **Write** your questions about how school life used to be different from today.

_____

- -

_____

_____

- -

_____

- -

_____

Step 3 **Ask** your questions.

Step 4 **Write** what you learned about how school used to be different from today.

_____

- -

_____

- -

_____

- -

_____

- -

_____

- -

_____

Step 5 **Think** about how to present your work. You may choose to create a recording of your interview or make a poster of a school from long ago.

Check In 1 > 2 > 3 > 4 >

Make Connections

 Talk about what the children in this photo are doing.

 Compare the photo to the text *Long Ago and Now.*

Quick Tip

Compare the photo and text using these sentence starters:

In the photo...

In Long Ago and Now...

Allan Cash Picture Library/Alamy Stock Photo

Check In 1 2 3 4

Write a Letter

1 **Look** at your Build Knowledge pages in your reader's notebook. What did you learn about life long ago?

2 **Write** a letter to a person who lived long ago and tell about the present. Include three examples of things you read about that have changed. Include an opening and a closing in your letter. Use two vocabulary words from the Word Bank.

3 **Draw** a picture to go with your letter.

Think about what you learned this week. Fill in the bars on page 117.

Build Knowledge

? Essential Question **How do we get our food?**

Build Vocabulary

 Talk with your partner about how we get our food.

 Write words about how we get food.

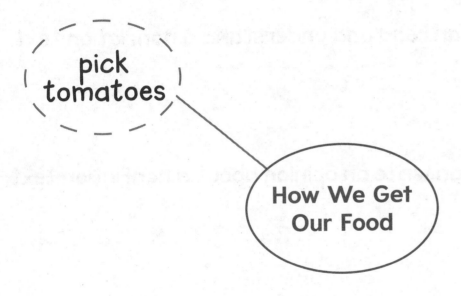

pick tomatoes

How We Get Our Food

My Goals

Think about what you know now. You'll learn a lot more this week. Fill in the bars.

Key

1 = I do not understand.

2 = I understand but need more practice.

3 = I understand.

4 = I understand and can teach someone.

What I Know Now

I can read and understand a nonfiction text.

1 > 2 > 3 > 4

I can write an opinion about a nonfiction text.

1 > 2 > 3 > 4

I know about different ways we get our food.

1 > 2 > 3 > 4

 You will come back to the next page later.

Think about what you've learned. Keep up the good work! Fill in the bars.

What I Learned

I can read and understand a nonfiction text.

1 > 2 > 3 > 4

I can write an opinion about a nonfiction text.

1 > 2 > 3 > 4

I know about different ways we get our food.

1 > 2 > 3 > 4

My Goal

I can read and understand a nonfiction text.

Find Text Evidence

Read to find out where breakfast foods come from.

Find the title. Point to each word in the title as you read it.

Essential Question

? How do we get our food?

A Look at Breakfast

Shared Read

 Find Text Evidence

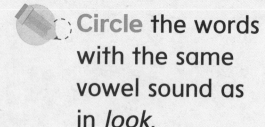 **Circle** the words with the same vowel sound as in *look*.

Make sure you understand how flour is made. Reread page 154 if you need to.

Bread is good for breakfast. But this isn't bread yet. It is wheat. Flour will be made from the wheat.

The wheat is crushed to make flour.

Bloomberg/Getty Images

First, dough is made. Next, the dough is shaped and baked. Then, it is done. It is bread. Last, the bread is put in bags.

Flour

NET WT 5LB (2.26mg)

Shared Read

Circle the words with the same vowel sound as in *look*.

Underline and read aloud the words *every* and *after*.

Grape jam is good on bread. But this isn't jam yet. It is a grape vine full of grapes.

Grapes grow on vines and then are picked when they are ripe.

Trucks take the grapes to a plant. Every grape is crushed to make mush. After that, the mush is cooked. Now, it is grape jam. Yum!

Shared Read

Find Text Evidence

Make sure you understand what happens at a plant. Look at the photo and reread page 159.

Talk about the steps for making orange juice.

Orange juice is good for breakfast, too! Lots and lots of sun makes oranges big and ripe. They will taste good. Soon, the big, ripe oranges will get pulled down.

Trucks take piles and piles of oranges to a plant. Then, they get washed. Next, they get crushed. Big sacks get filled with juice.

Find Text Evidence

Underline and read aloud the words *buy* and *work*.

Reread any parts you do not understand before you retell the text.

The food is shipped in trucks to shops. It is stacked up. Now, it is for sale. People will buy it and bring it home. It will make a good breakfast!

(t) Mark Richardson/Alamy Stock Photo; (b) Ariel Skelley/Blend Images/Getty Images

It takes work to make food for breakfast.

Food	Where It Comes From	How It Is Made
bread	wheat	Wheat is crushed into flour. Dough is made. Dough is baked into bread.
grape jam	grapes	Grapes are crushed to make mush. Mush is cooked into jam.
orange juice	oranges	Oranges are crushed into juice.

Writing Practice

Write Sentences

 Talk about where food comes from.

 Listen to these sentences about food.

> Apples are my favorite fruit.
> An apple isn't too sweet.
> It is crisp and yummy!

 Underline the reasons for the opinion.

 Stretch the sounds in the words as you read them.

Writing Trait

Reasons for an opinion are details that help the reader understand why it is your opinion.

Talk about your favorite food.

 Write sentences about your favorite food. Give reasons for your opinion.

_____

- -

_____

- -

_____

- -

_____

Underline the reasons for your opinion.

Stretch the sounds in the words as you write them.

Writing Skill

Remember to stretch the sounds in words you write. This will help you hear the beginning, middle, and end sounds.

Nonfiction gives facts about real things. It can use photos and captions to give more information.

A Look at Breakfast

Reread to find out what makes this a nonfiction text.

Talk about what you see in the photos.

Write two facts from the text. Then write what else you learn from the photos and captions.

Check In 1 > 2 > 3 > 4 >

Facts from Text	Information from Captions and Photos

Authors sometimes use time order when writing nonfiction. Words such as *first, next, then,* and *last* can help you understand the time order. Details in a text can give us information about the time order of events.

 Reread page 155 of "A Look at Breakfast."

 Talk about how bread is made.

 Write the steps the chef uses for making bread on page 155.

Check In 1 > 2 > 3 > 4 >

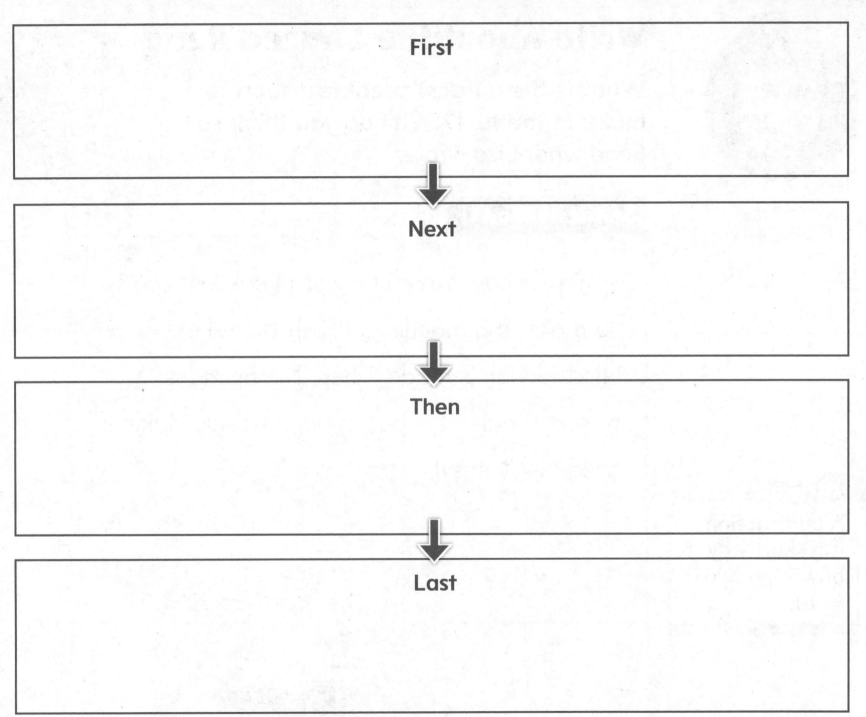

First

Next

Then

Last

Lisa

Write About the Shared Read

What is the hardest breakfast food to make in the text? Why do you think so? Read what Lisa wrote.

Student Model

I think bread is the hardest breakfast food to make. Big machines crush the wheat. Next, dough is made. Then, the bread is baked. Finally, it is put in bags to sell. Making bread isn't easy!

Grammar

A **contraction** is a short way of writing two words.

Talk about details Lisa used from the text. Underline the reasons for her opinion.

Circle the contraction.

Stretch the sounds in words as you read.

Write what you notice about Lisa's writing.

Quick Tip

You can talk about Lisa's writing using these sentence starters:

I noticed . . .
Lisa used . . .

Respond to the Anchor Text

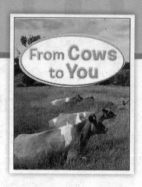

From Cows to You

 Retell the text using the photos and words from the text.

✏️ **Write** about the text.

What can farmers do to make sure people want to buy their milk?

Text Evidence

Page

_____

- - - - - - - - - - - - - - - - - - -

_____

- - - - - - - - - - - - - - - - - - -

_____

How are small farms and big farms different?

Text Evidence

Page

- - - - - - - - - - - - - - - - - - -

_____

_____

- - - - - - - - - - - - - - - - - - -

_____

Check In   1 ⟩ 2 ⟩ 3 ⟩ 4 ⟩

Talk about what you see in the photos on page 96.

Write what the text says about the photos.

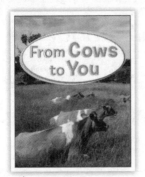

What the Photos Show	What the Text Says

What do the photos help you understand?

_____

_____

_____

Talk about the information on pages 96–99.

 Write about each step that happens to get milk from cows to us.

1.	2.	3.	4.

What does the author want you to understand?

_____

- -

_____

- -

_____

Check In   1 ⟩ 2 ⟩ 3 ⟩ 4 ⟩

Writing and Grammar

Write About the Anchor Text

Based on *From Cows to You,* which job in the milk process would you rather have? Why?

 Talk about the question.

 Write your answer below.

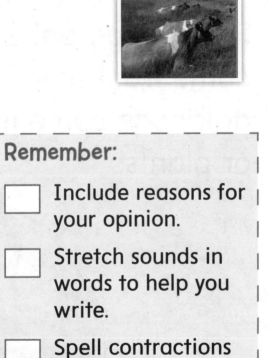

_____

- -

_____

- -

_____

- -

_____

- -

_____

Remember:

☐ Include reasons for your opinion.

☐ Stretch sounds in words to help you write.

☐ Spell contractions correctly.

Check In 1 2 3 4

The Five Food Groups

The five food groups are dairy, grains, fruits, vegetables, and protein.

Fruits, vegetables, and grains come from plants. Protein and dairy can come from animals or plants.

Read to find out about the food groups.

Circle the words that name the five food groups.

Talk about why you think the author tells where foods come from.

JGI/Jamie Grill/Blend Images/Getty Images

Do you eat food from every group? Let's take a look at the diagram to help you find out!

dairy

vegetables

grains

protein

fruit

 Circle your favorite food in the diagram. Tell which food group it belongs to.

 Talk about how the diagram can help you understand the five food groups.

Talk About It

How is a food diagram helpful for a reader?

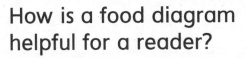
Check In   1   2   3   4

DebbiSmirnoff/E+/Getty Images

Investigate a Food

Step 1 Choose a food to learn about.

_____

- -

_____

Step 2 Write questions about where your food
comes from.

_____

- -

_____

- -

_____

- -

_____

Step 3 Use tables of contents to find the information
you need. Read for answers to your questions.

Step 4 Write what you learned about your food.
Put the information in the correct sequence.

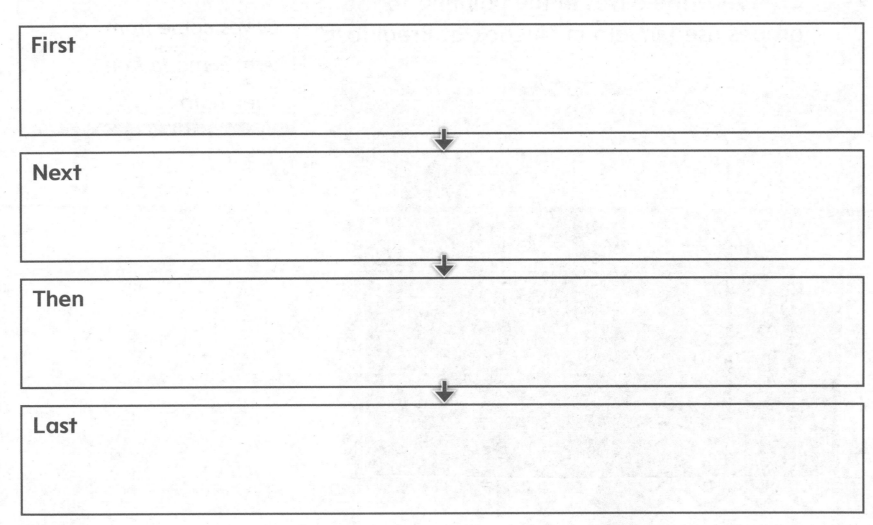

First

Next

Then

Last

Step 5 Choose how to present your work.

Talk about the painting. What does it tell you about where olives come from?

 Compare the olives in the painting to the grapes used in jam in "A Look at Breakfast."

Quick Tip

You can compare using these sentence starters:

Olives come from . . .

Jam is made from . . .

They both . . .

Courtesy National Gallery of Art, Washington

This painting shows workers picking olives.

Check In 1 2 3 4

Write a Nonfiction Text

1 **Look** at your Build Knowledge pages in your reader's notebook. What did you learn about how we get our food?

2 **Write** about two of the workers who help us get food. Write about how they do their jobs and how we get our food. Use text evidence. Use two vocabulary words from the Word Bank.

3 **Draw** a picture to go with your writing.

Think about what you learned this week. Fill in the bars on page 151.

Writing and Grammar

Danica

I wrote a nonfiction text. It is about real things and events. I found facts about my topic in books.

Student Model

Nonfiction

My nonfiction text has facts and information.

Wrist Watches

People did not always wear wrist watches.

How did people check the time long ago?

They had to dig watches out of their pockets.

180 Unit 3

But soldiers needed to check the time quickly. So they tied watches to their wrists. It's much easier checking the time with a wrist watch!

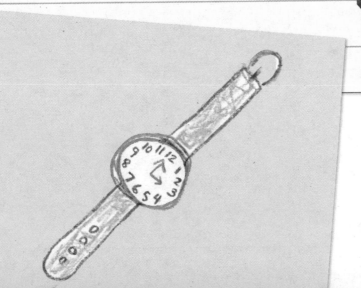

Genre

 Talk about what makes Danica's text nonfiction.

 Ask any questions you have.

 Circle a fact about something real.

Brainstorm and Plan

 Talk about ideas for your nonfiction text.

 Draw some of your ideas.

Quick Tip

As you brainstorm ideas, think about topics you are interested in and know a lot about.

Choose a nonfiction topic to write about.
Choose something you know about.

_____

- -

_____

Find facts about your topic. Write facts
about your topic from the texts.

_____

- -

_____

_____

- -

_____

Circle what makes your text nonfiction.

Writing and Grammar

Draft

Read Danica's draft of her nonfiction text.

Organization

I began with the topic. Then I wrote more about that idea.

Student Model

Wrist Watches

People did not always wear wrist watches.

How did people check the time long ago?

They had to dig watches out of their pockets.

Writing Skill

I used endings like **-ed** and **-ing** correctly.

Important Facts

I included important facts about my topic.

But soldiers needed to check the time.

So they tied watches to their wrists.

Your Turn

Begin to write your nonfiction text. Use your ideas from pages 182–183. Make sure to include a topic and important facts.

Check In 1 2 3 4

Writing and Grammar

Revise and Edit

Think about how Danica revised and edited her nonfiction text.

I spelled high frequency words correctly.

Student Model

Wrist Watches

People did not always wear wrist watches.

How did people check the time long ago?

They had to dig watches out of their pockets.

I made sure to use past-tense verbs correctly.

I revised by adding a detail to give more information.

But soldiers needed to check the time quickly.
So they tied watches to their wrists. It's much easier checking the time with a wrist watch!

Concluding Statement

I added more information to make my ending more interesting.

Your Turn

Revise and edit your writing in your writer's notebook. Include a strong concluding statement. Be sure to use verbs correctly.

Check In   1 2 3 4

Publish and Present

 Finish editing your writing. Make sure it is neat and ready to publish.

 Practice presenting your work with a partner. Use this checklist.

 Present your work.

Review Your Work	Yes	No
Speaking and Listening		
I paid attention to the tone of my piece.	☐	☐
I spoke loudly and clearly.	☐	☐
I listened carefully.	☐	☐
I used complete sentences.	☐	☐

Talk with a partner about what you did well in your writing.

What did you do well in your writing?

_____

- -

_____

_____

- -

_____

What do you need to work on?

_____

- -

_____

_____

- -

_____

 Think about your goal of writing a nonfiction text. Fill in the bars.

Watch It Grow

 Listen to "Twinsies."

 Talk about how Birch Seed and Pine Seed are alike.

 Draw ways Birch Seed and Pine Seed are different.

Share your drawing with a partner. Talk about how the trees feel about being different.

Write about how the seeds change as they grow.

Quick Tip

You can use these sentence starters:

The trees both . . .
Then, they discover . . .

_____

- -

_____

- -

_____

- -

_____

Check In 1 2 3 4

Connect to Science

Observe a Plant

 Talk about a plant you would like to observe.

What to do

1. **Observe** a plant you can find near your school.

2. **Draw** a picture of your plant.

3. **Add** details and labels to the picture.

4. **Compare** your plant to a partner's plant.

5. **Write** about what you observed.

You need

pencil

crayons

What you observe

My observations

Write a Friendly Letter

You can share news or feelings with a friend by writing a friendly letter.

 Look and listen to this friendly letter.

The **greeting** tells who the letter is for.

Write your news in the **body** of the letter.

The **closing** tells who the note is from.

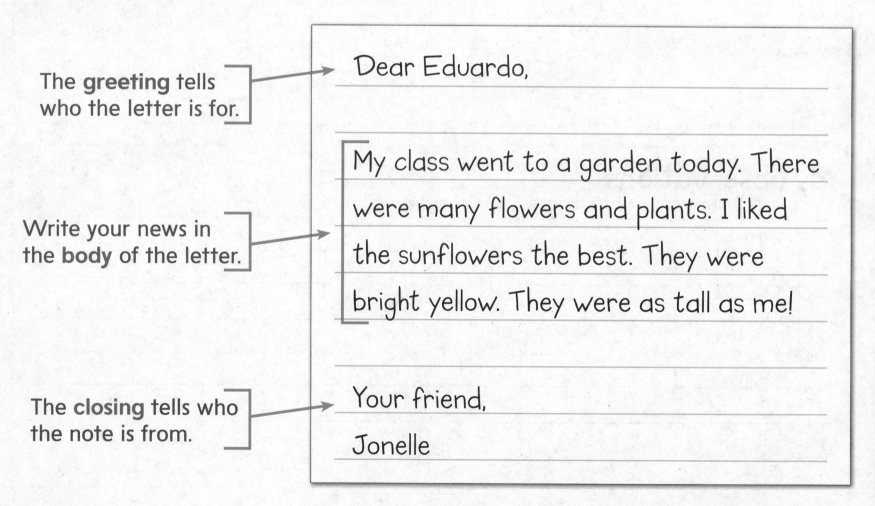

Dear Eduardo,

My class went to a garden today. There were many flowers and plants. I liked the sunflowers the best. They were bright yellow. They were as tall as me!

Your friend,

Jonelle

Talk about a friendly letter you would like to write about your favorite flower or plant.

 Write your friendly letter.

Dear _____,

_____

_____

_____

From,

_____

Extend Your Learning

Choose Your Own Book

Tell a partner about a book you want to read. Say why you want to read it.

Minutes I Read

Write the title.

_____

- - - - - - - - - - - - - - - - - - -

_____

Write about the book. What was it about? Did you like it? Why or why not?

_____

- - - - - - - - - - - - - - - - - - -

_____

- - - - - - - - - - - - - - - - - - -

_____

- - - - - - - - - - - - - - - - - - -

_____

Think About Your Learning

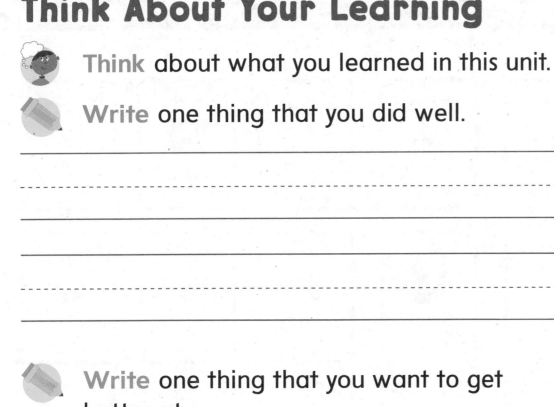

Think about what you learned in this unit.

Write one thing that you did well.

_____

_____

_____

Write one thing that you want to get better at.

_____

_____

_____

Share a goal you have with your partner.

My Sound-Spellings

Aa a	**Bb** b	**Cc** c ck k	**Dd** d _ed	**Ee** e ea	**Ff** f ph	**Gg** g
apple	bat	camel	dolphin	egg	fire	guitar
Hh h_	**Ii** i	**Jj** j dge ge gi_	**Kk** c k ck	**Ll** l _le	**Mm** m	**Nn** n kn_ gn
hippo	insect	jump	koala	lemon	map	nest
Oo o	**Pp** p	**Qq** qu_	**Rr** r wr_	**Ss** s ce ci_	**Tt** _t _ed	**Uu** u
octopus	piano	queen	rose	sun	turtle	umbrella
Vv v	**Ww** w_	**Xx** x	**Yy** y_	**Zz** z _s		
volcano	window	box	yo-yo	zipper		

th	sh	ch tch	wh_	ng	a ai_ _ay a_e ea ei	i y i_e igh ie
thumb	shell	cheese	whale	sing	train	five

o oa ow o_e _oe	u u_e _ew _ue	e_e ea ee e _y ie _ey	ar	er ir ur or	oar or ore	ow ou
boat	cube	tree	star	shirt	corn	cow

oi _oy	oo_	oo u_e u _ew ue ou ui	a aw au augh al	air are ear ere
boy	book	spoon	straw	chair

Aa Bb Cc Dd Ee

Ff Gg Hh Ii Jj

Kk Ll Mm Nn

Oo Pp Qq Rr

Ss Tt Uu Vv

Ww Xx Yy Zz